D1020170

115952996

NURSING

NURSING

Blythe Camenson

VGM Career Horizons
a division of NTC Publishing Group
Lincolnwood, Illinois USA

Dedication

To Linda Dickinson, Silvia Pio, Ellen Raphaeli, and my editor, Sarah Kennedy, for their special nurturing talents.

Photo Credits:
Pages 1, 15, 29, and 43: Photo Network, Tustin, CA; page 57: Jean Clough; page 71: American Nurses' Association.
All other photographs courtesy of the author.

Library of Congress Cataloging-in-Publication Data

Camenson, Blythe.
    Career Portraits, nursing / Blythe Camenson.
        p.   cm. — (VGM's career portraits)
    Includes index.
    ISBN 0-8442-4369-8
    1. Nursing—Vocational guidance—Juvenile literature.
    [1. Nursing—Vocational guidance. 2. Vocational guidance.]
    I. Title. II. Series: VGM professional careers series.
    RT82.C225 1995   94-42628
    610.73'06'9—dc20   CIP
                                      AC

Published by VGM Career Horizons, a division of NTC Publishing Group
4255 West Touhy Avenue
Lincolnwood (Chicago), Illinois 60646-1975, U.S.A.
© 1995 by NTC Publishing Group. All rights reserved.
No part of this book may be reproduced, stored in a retrieval system,
or transmitted in any form or by any means,
electronic, mechanical, photocopying, recording or otherwise,
without the prior permission of NTC Publishing Group.
Manufactured in the United States of America.

5 6 7 8 9 0 QB 9 8 7 6 5 4 3 2 1

Contents

And always keep a-hold of Nurse,
For fear of finding something worse.

Hilaire Pierre Belloc
Cautionary Tales, 'Jim'

Introduction

To choose a career in nursing means you have a special gift. You sincerely care about people and you know how to show those feelings. Your patients might be frightened, in pain, or seriously ill, but under your care they sense your warmth and concern and feel comforted by it.

Nurses love working with people, all kinds of people. Your patients might be rich or poor, young or old, from a variety of backgrounds and cultures.

As a nurse you have many different options. In a traditional hospital setting you can work with newborn infants and children, in the emergency room, or in the intensive care unit. You can assist at a birth, during an operation, or provide counseling for psychiatric patients.

You also can work in a private counseling center, an elementary school, or a university infirmary. Some nurses choose to work in their patients' homes, in a sports clinic, aboard a cruise ship, or at a summer camp. Other nurses work in nursing homes, or even in prisons.

Nurses can be administrators and educators—directing the care given in a hospital department or teaching future nurses the skills they'll need in this rewarding career.

Training for nurses can take from two to four years, or even longer, as more and more professionals go on to earn advanced degrees. The choice is yours, so let's start exploring the exciting and challenging profession of nursing!

CAREERS

IN

HOSPITALS

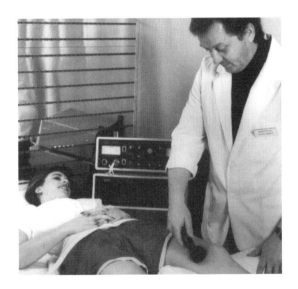

O nce you have become an RN, there is a wide
range of career opportunities open to you.
Approximately 68 percent of all nurses work in
hospital settings. These are dedicated men and women
who put in long, hard hours, most of which they spend
on their feet, standing, bending, stooping, and briskly
walking countless miles of hospital corridors every day,
taking care of the needs of their patients.

Within a hospital setting you have a variety of departments to choose from: you can work with newborn
infants in the nursery, with patients recovering from

1

surgery, or with patients suffering from terminal illnesses. During your nursing training, you will have the opportunity to get a taste of the different possibilities and to find the area of nursing that appeals to you the most. This book will introduce you to several challenging nursing careers and the nurses who work in them.

How you can become a nurse

At present, there are four different ways you can become a registered nurse, or RN:

1. Through a two-year community college, earning an associate's degree in nursing;
2. Through a three-year hospital-based nursing school, earning a diploma;
3. Through a four-year university program, resulting in the bachelor of science degree in nursing (BSN); and
4. For those who have a bachelor's degree in a different subject, there is a "generic" master's degree in nursing, a two- to three-year program beyond the bachelor's degree.

Today, and certainly in the future, the BSN is considered the minimum qualification for a satisfying career. The two-year associate's degree and the three-year hospital-based diploma programs are closing down quickly throughout the country and student nurses are being encouraged to enroll in four-year universities.

For many nursing specialties, it is essential to earn a master's degree or an advanced certificate; and for some nurses, those who wish to teach, a PhD, or doctor of philosophy, in nursing is required.

After your schooling, you will be expected to take a licensing exam, for the basic RN and any specialty areas you might choose.

What it's like working in a hospital

Most nurses choose a career in hospital nursing because they love the "hands-on" contact with their patients. Generally, they work with people who are very sick, recovering from surgery, or suffering with a variety of illnesses and diseases.

Their main concern is to make their patients as comfortable as possible. They work with a variety of patients and ailments, providing direct care and assisting physicians and surgeons with their activities. Often, they work as part of a team with other professionals—physical therapists, x-ray technicians, nurse practitioners, and other nurses.

Which hospital department would you prefer?

The Emergency Room (ER): Patients come in from the street, on their own, or they are brought in by the police or paramedics. They can be suffering from a variety of traumas—anything from a broken bone, gunshot wound, or serious burn to a heart attack or a stroke.

Intensive Care Unit (ICU)/ Cardiac Care Unit (CCU): Patients are in critical condition and require more intensive, one-on-one care.

Medical/Surgical: Patients are suffering from a variety of illnesses and ailments or are recovering from surgery.

Obstetrics and Gynecology (OB/GYN): Here you'll find the maternity ward, where women deliver their babies, and the nursery, for new-born infants. Women also are admitted to this part of the hospital for surgery or other procedures.

The Operating Room (OR): Sur-geons, OR nurses, nurse anesthe-tists, and other professional staff work as a team during operations.

Outpatient Departments/Clinics: Patients are seen who are not sick enough to be admitted to the hospital. They might need a follow-up visit to check their medication, or to have physical therapy or a session with a counselor.

Pediatrics: Hospital staff are trained in the diseases and other problems of children.

Psychiatric Ward: Patients are suffering from a variety of emotional problems or illnesses, such as depression or schizophrenia.

The pleasures and pressures of hospital nursing

Hospital nursing is hard work, but often can be rewarding. Nothing makes a nurse happier than to see a patient who was seriously ill recover and go home to lead a normal life. However, that doesn't happen always and a hospital nurse has to be prepared to deal with the death of a patient.

The work schedule is one of the job's most difficult aspects. Hospital nurses are expected to rotate shifts. Although generally they work 40 hours a week, those hours could fall in the middle of the night, on weekends, or on holidays.

Salaries for hospital nurses

Hospital floor nurses are among the lowest paid of all nursing professionals. It is obvious that floor nurses are not doing the job for the money—they love their work and the patient contact.

Is a career in nursing right for you?

Do you really want to be a nurse? Or should you become doctor? It's easy to make a mistake when choosing between these two related fields. If you like the scientific aspect—running tests or doing dissections—then medicine is the career you should choose. But if you like concerning yourself with healthy foods, exercise, doing all the right things to stay healthy, and you like to teach, then nursing should be your career.

Let's Meet...

Heidi Rubin
Cardiac Rehabilitation Nurse

Heidi works in an outpatient department of a large hospital, taking care of patients recovering from a heart attack or open-heart surgery. Her reward is watching a patient get stronger and able to return to an active lifestyle.

What drew you to cardiac rehabilitation nursing?

Initially, I started out with a career in exercise therapy, teaching aerobics, body sculpting, and prenatal classes. But then I realized in my mid-twenties that I was not going to be able to jump about so physically all my life. Your knees start to go and then you experience all types of aches and pains. It was time to consider something else. Financially, I couldn't depend on the exercise therapy career for my retirement down the road. First I considered physical therapy, then I chose nursing. I wanted a career where I could help people and use my previous experience.

What does your work involve?

I provide follow-up care for heart patients on an outpatient basis. The whole purpose is to help them get their strength back. When I get a new patient I do an initial assessment. I look at his wound, get his medical history—if he's diabetic or has hypertension (high blood pressure), for example—and determine his grip strength and his strength in general. Then I put him on an exercise program using treadmills, stationary bicycles, or Stepmasters, depending on the needs of each patient.

In addition to exercise therapy, I provide information about their disease, the possibility of re-occurrence, lifestyle changes they might have to make, and their diet, among other things.

What kind of special training would someone need to do your job?

In addition to my experience in exercise therapy, I have an associate's degree in nursing. Someone also should have at least two years' critical care nursing experience in cardiology and an understanding of exercise physiology and exercise technology.

What do you like most/least about your job?

It's rewarding to see that the patient has gotten back into his lifestyle. They come to me in a frightened and debilitated state. It's wonderful to see them three months later walk out the door for the last time, smiling and happy.

What I like least is that often I take care of more than one person at a time—I run classes and could have up to 11 patients in one hour. That's a lot of stress. But I do love my work; I don't think I'd ever go back to floor nursing.

A Bittersweet Moment for Heidi

A couple of years ago Heidi had a patient who was having a dangerous cardiac arrhythmia, his heart was not beating the way it should have been beating. She had taken care of him for several days, though she hadn't been assigned to him on that particular day.

When she heard he was in trouble she ran into the room to provide assistance. He looked up at her and told her how glad he was to see her. He thanked her for being so nice to him. And the only thing Heidi could do was hold his hand. She couldn't find her voice because her emotions were running over.

As a nurse, Heidi was told to be careful not to get too involved personally with her patients, but she did care about him and it was hard for her.

He died holding Heidi's hand. That memory will stay with her always.

Let's Meet...

Bertha Lovelace
Nurse Anesthetist

Bertha is the chief nurse anesthetist at the Cleveland Clinic. She works in operating rooms and is responsible for keeping patients free of pain during surgery.

What does a nurse anesthetist do?

A nurse anesthetist is responsible for keeping the patient anesthetized and free of pain during an operation. She or he also is responsible for bringing the patient back to a state of wakefulness afterward. Generally, we use sodium pentothal or other medications, called inhalation agents, or breathing agents.

Before a patient's surgery we meet with him, in a pre-operative clearance, to ask about his physical well-being, any history of surgery or encounters with anesthetics, if he has any allergies, and when he ate last. During the surgery we monitor the patient's vital signs and adjust the anesthetic according to the patient response.

Since I am the chief nurse anesthetist, I am also a clinical instructor of student nurses. We work as part of a team, designing a plan for the patient with the anesthesiologist (MD). The anesthesiologists act as the directors of the operating rooms, and in addition to the OR nurse and the surgeon, there is a nurse anesthetist with the patient at all times.

What are the rewards of your profession?

I get a sense of success after each operation, knowing I kept the patient pain-free and then was able to awaken him in a timely fashion. I contribute a major part to the patient's comfort level.

Also, you are working with a team of decision-making people. You have to be able to make split-second decisions; there's not a lot of leeway. It's stimulating. And because we're a teaching hospital, we're always learning something new.

Also I like that it's one-on-one patient care. You deal with one case at a time. This career offers a challenge that regular floor nursing didn't offer me.

There also is a nice financial reward. Salaries for nurse anesthetists are 40 to 50 percent higher than for floor nurses.

Are there any pressures to your job?

The pressures are entwined with the pleasures. Every patient responds differently so you must be on your toes, thinking about your next step—if you need to give more anesthesia, for example. There's also pressure when you work with very sick patients. Then your anesthesia has to be customized.

What kind of training do nurse anesthetists receive?

Altogether, you need seven and a half years of training and experience before you can become a nurse anesthetist. That includes a four-year bachelor's program in nursing, one year of critical care experience, and the two-and-one-half year nurse anesthetist program.

A Typical Day for Bertha Lovelace

Bertha starts her day around 9 A.M. The first hour or so of her shift she spends on administrative duties, scheduling the different nurses she supervises or returning phone calls. Around 11 in the morning she puts on her scrubs and mask (and makes sure she is wearing comfortable shoes) and enters the operating room. Until approximately 2:00 P.M. she relieves the working nurse anesthetists, one at a time, for lunch. Before they take their breaks, they report to Bertha on the patients' condition, blood pressure, and other vital signs. Also they tell her what different anesthetic agents are being used.

At 2 o'clock she checks on all the rooms and finds out when the operations will finish up. Then, she spends time scheduling another team of nurse anesthetists to take over the operations still in progress.

For the rest of the day, Bertha might step in and provide more relief for dinner breaks or schedule nurses for "add ons" or emergency surgery. Also she provides training for student nurse anesthetists who are present in the operating room. Bertha finishes up her day any time between 5 o'clock and 6:30 P.M.

Success Stories

Florence Nightingale Florence Nightingale is a familiar name. Although English, she was born in Italy in 1820. Because of her dedication to helping war victims, she is considered to be the founder of modern nursing. She was also a pioneer in stressing the importance of sanitation and hygiene.

Florence Nightingale received only a short term of nursing training during the 1850s. There was a war going on—the Crimean War—and her services were needed desperately by the British Army.

Her nursing care in Turkey and the Crimea revolutionized army medical care. Because of her concern about sanitation and hygiene, she was responsible for lowering the death rate. Also she set the standard for proper nursing practice that is followed today.

In 1860 Florence Nightingale established a school for training nurses. Her methods became a model for modern nursing training.

She wrote several important books, including one called *Notes on Matters Affecting the Health, Efficiency, and Hospital Administration of the British Army.*

Florence Nightingale was the first woman ever to be awarded the British Order of Merit.

Find Out More

You and nursing

There are many factors to consider when deciding upon a specific path in nursing, and though for many salary is not the most important issue, it should be taken into account. Here is a chart that tells you the approximate yearly salaries of nurses in different specialties. These are average salaries. Depending upon the area of the country or in which setting you work, the salaries could be higher or lower. The chart also shows that most salaries go up with the more education you have.

	Associate's Degree	3-Year Diploma	BSN	Master's	Doctorate
Administrator	$39,000	$41,000	$45,000	$54,000	—
Supervisor	$36,700	$37,100	$42,000	$45,000	—
Instructor	$31,700	$35,300	$35,300	$37,200	$45,000
Nurse Manager	$38,200	$40,100	$43,000	$46,000	
Staff/Floor Nurse	$34,000	$35,000	$36,500	$41,500	—
Nurse Practitioner/ Midwife	$38,700	$38,700	$41,700	$45,300	—
Certified Nurse Anesthetist	$76,000	$78,000	$80,000	—	—
Clinical Specialist	$36,700	$37,800	$41,000	$44,200	—

— Not enough information available

To find out more about nursing careers contact:

American Association of Critical
   Care Nurses
101 Columbia
Aliso Viejo, CA 92656–1491

American Nurses Association
600 Maryland Avenue, SW
Suite 100W
Washington, DC 20024–2571

Association of Rehabilitation
   Nurses
5700 Old Orchard Road, First
   Floor
Skokie, IL 60077–1057

National Federation of Specialty
   Nursing Organizations
875 Kings Highway
Deptford, NJ 08096

National Student Nurses'
   Association
555 West 57th Street
New York, NY 10019

CAREERS
WITH
FAMILIES

N urses who choose to work with families have several different options they can follow. They can have their own private practice, just as a doctor does, or they can work as part of a team in hospitals and clinics. Jobs are available in large cities or rural villages—nurses working with families can find employment anywhere. Their patients range from pregnant women and newborn infants to fathers and grandparents, and everyone in between.

The two careers this section focuses on—nurse midwife and nurse practitioner—provide a high degree of professional independence, as well as personal satisfaction.

Duties of nurse midwives and nurse practitioners

Nurse midwives approach pregnancy as a normal condition. They emphasize counseling, information, and support. They have more time to spend with their patients than physicians do. A midwife is there with the patient throughout labor, while many physicians only are able to attend the actual birth.

Midwives are trained to recognize complications, and if any should occur, an obstetrician, the physician who is trained to handle these abnormal situations, is consulted and they work together to ensure the patients' well-being.

The nurse practitioner profession was designed more than thirty years ago to provide health care to those who didn't have access to physicians. And in some settings today, in rural villages, for example, nurse practitioners are the only providers. They are licensed legally to prescribe medication in most states, and trained to fill in for pediatricians, obstetricians, and general practice physicians. In urban areas, practitioners work with physicians, providing a comprehensive health care package.

Practitioners focus their attention on a patient's common problems, freeing up time for the physician who is trained to correct more serious ailments. Nurse practitioners are not as disease-oriented; they try to prevent diseases, and if a disease is not correctable immediately, they teach patients how to live with it.

Job settings for nurse midwives and nurse practitioners

Nurse midwives and nurse practitioners find work in city hospitals, clinics, and private doctors' offices; in rural areas, such as on Indian reservations, in Alaska, or in the Appalachian Mountains; or around the world with the armed forces or the Foreign Service.

They also can, in much the same way a doctor does, set up their own office and work in private practice. Some nurse midwives and nurse practitioners even make home visits.

Training for nurse midwives and practitioners

Nurse midwives and nurse practitioners study in special programs above the RN or BSN, receiving master's degrees and additional training. They take special licensing exams for their specialties.

The rewards, the pay, and the perks

Because there is a great demand for nurse midwives and nurse practitioners, salaries are high, if not the highest in the nursing profession. A midwife or practitioner can go into private practice and make about the same salary a doctor would with a general practice. This can run to six figures, but it depends on the area of the country in which you live and how much competition there is.

Nurse midwives or practitioners who join the armed forces start out at a high military rank and receive all the accompanying benefits. Large private companies, such as the oil or computer industries with 1,000 or more employees, prefer to hire midwives and practitioners rather than MDs. They can afford to pay attractive salaries, but they still save money.

As one certified nurse midwife put it, "What could be more rewarding than job satisfaction *and* good money?"

The job outlook

The job outlook for nurse midwives and nurse practitioners is excellent. With all the health care reform being planned, eventually physicians won't make as much money performing normal, routine duties. Their skills will be left to surgery and other complicated procedures. The skills of midwives and practitioners will be utilized more. In essence, costs will be kept down and everyone will save money.

But cost is not the only factor ensuring a good job outlook. There are many regions in the country that don't attract enough physicians. There are some patient populations, such as the elderly or inner city teens, that are being neglected. Midwives and practitioners are in even more demand to fill positions in these areas.

Getting a head start

The Red Cross offers a course for babysitters and teaches CPR and other first aid skills. Volunteer your time, visit babies in nurseries, and read as much as you can about the different careers. An informed choice is the best choice.

ℒet's ℳeet...

Stephie ℳorin
Certified ℕurse ℳidwife

Stephie has been a certified nurse midwife (RN, CNM) since 1986. She feels it's a great honor to take care of women and see them go from the early stages of pregnancy to becoming a mother.

What made you decide to become a midwife?

When I was just out of high school I met a nurse who was going to become a nurse midwife. That was the first time I had heard of the career. At the same time, a woman I knew was going to have a baby and I got to be at the birth. It just clicked and I knew that's what I wanted to do.

What does a nurse midwife do?

A nurse midwife is trained in all areas of normal obstetrics, well-woman gynecological care, care of the newborn, and care of normal healthy women throughout their childbearing cycle, and afterward, too. In the United States, most midwives work in hospitals, birthing centers, and home care.

I work with a group of other midwives. Our midwifery service is employed by the hospital and we work with a group of physicians. Occasionally I travel to various community-based health centers, but all the births I attend are in the hospital.

A woman comes in for prenatal care at the health center. She'll see me for her first visit, which I hope will be early on in her pregnancy. I'll take a health history and I'll spend time getting to know her, giving her information about our service, and about her pregnancy. I'll do some blood work, a physical exam, decide if any tests are needed, make any referrals—to a nutritionist, for example, or sometimes to a social worker—then I'll set up her next visit with me.

During follow-up appointments we talk about how she's feeling, if the baby's moving yet—and we listen to the baby's heart and measure the belly to see how it's growing.

When my patient goes into labor, either I or one of my coworkers will meet her at the hospital. We'll evaluate her baby and her labor with different monitoring devices. We support her through the different stages of labor—a nurse will be there, too, and a doctor always is available in case of complications. If the woman wants any medication, we're able to give it to her.

After the baby is born, we have follow-up visits to teach her about newborn care and what to expect from her body as she recovers from the delivery.

What kind of training does a midwife need?

There are different ways to become a midwife. My program at Yale combined an RN with midwifery training and a master's degree in nursing. If you're not a nurse when you start the program it takes three years.

Stephie's First Delivery

When Stephie was 18 years old, she attended the birth of her friend's baby. It was the one event that made her decide to become a midwife.

Stephie's friend wanted to have a more natural delivery than was common at that time. She wanted her friends there in addition to the baby's father, and wanted someone there to take pictures. Stephie was invited because her friend knew she was interested in health care.

She stood at the foot of the bed with another friend of hers—who passed out. There was soft music playing, and natural light—no bright, artificial lights.

The actual birth astounded Stephie. She was moved profoundly. Looking back, she realized that she wasn't moved toward wanting to have a baby (although she has one now), but more toward helping other people have babies.

Stephie was amazed at the power of birth. She remembers thinking it was incredible that there had been six people in the room, then all of a sudden there were seven. But no one had walked in the door.

It changed her life.

Let's Meet...

Brad Potts
Nurse Practitioner

Brad has a BSN and a MS in primary care. He loves being able to work with the whole family and to focus on people who are in good health.

What does a nurse practitioner do?

A nurse practitioner evaluates a patient's total health care needs. My patients are anywhere from two weeks old to elderly. Initially, we do a head-to-toe physical and a complete health assessment. If a patient comes in with a specific complaint that's complicated and would require intervention, we can refer him or her to a physician, or if it's a common health problem, we can handle it ourselves.

What made you choose a family practice?

I like being able to take care of the whole family—the newborns, mom and dad, grandmom and granddad, aunts and uncles, and sisters and brothers—because health care is more than just the individual. Where you come from, the culture you're in, the beliefs of your parents or grandparents— it's all a big influence. If one

person is sick, it affects everybody. When I
know what's going on in the family, it helps
me deal with all the family members. If a
baby is sick, for example, and I'm seeing
Grandmother, I know she might be upset
about the baby and might not be sleeping
well.

Are there any pressures to your work?

There are too many people to see and not
enough time to spend with them, so you can
feel pulled from all directions. It's a universal problem. So many people need health
care and there are just not enough people
or time to take care of everyone the way
you'd like.

And the paperwork is terrible. You have
to document everything. You worry about
medical/legal issues. You don't want to end
up in court. I have malpractice insurance
through my job, but I carry an additional
policy for more protection. These days,
everyone seems to be lawsuit-happy and
anyone who had any contact, even if they
just said "hello," could be named in the
lawsuit. It's gotten out of hand.

It's Not Always a Man's World

Being a nurse, who happens to be a man, can cause some awkward moments. Brad says an obstacle that he's always trying to overcome is that he's not a male nurse, he's a nurse practitioner and sees all patients, men and women.

In nursing school he was assigned to male patients. Brad used to have to ask to get a female patient assignment.

Brad says that sometimes, because he's a male, patients assume he must be a doctor. He's always correcting that impression—he thinks it's important that people understand the difference between doctors and nurses. But he's more likely to run into discrimination by his colleagues—female nurses—than by his patients.

A male will come in with a sore throat, for example, and a female colleague will assign him to Brad. If a female came in with a sore throat, she'd be referred to the other nurse practitioner he works with, a female.

Brad talks to his colleagues on a regular basis about this. Initially, he had to do it every day. He still has to address the problem at least once a month.

The advantage he sees to being a man who is a nurse is that he can be a role model for young men. Oftentimes, a male might think that he'd like to be a nurse, but because it's not what men *usually do,* he might shy away. At least they can see Brad out there, a typical man, who has chosen nursing as his career.

Success Stories

Planned Parenthood Federation of America

The Planned Parenthood Federation of America, known as Planned Parenthood for short, was founded by Margaret Sanger in 1921. The organization's goal was to provide the general public with information on family planning. Today, there are clinics in almost every major city in the country, and thousands of women each year benefit from the support and information the professionally trained counselors offer.

Margaret Sanger

Margaret Sanger was born in New York in 1883 and coined the term "birth control." In fact, she was the leader of the birth-control movement in this country. Working as a nurse in the slums of New York City, she was horrified by the deaths from illegal abortions. She opened a birth-control clinic in Brooklyn, but was arrested for "creating a public nuisance." Her struggle with the law created much public attention and added drama to the cause. Ultimately, she won the right for doctors to give family-planning information to their patients.

Margaret Sanger was the first president of the International Planned Parenthood Federation in 1953. She died in 1966.

Find Out More

You and working with families

Ask yourself the following questions to assess if you have what it takes to make a good nurse midwife or nurse practitioner:

- Am I good with my hands?
- Can people read my handwriting?
- Do I enjoy studying science?
- Am I able to keep track of my activities in writing? (Do I keep a journal or diary, for example?)
- Am I willing to learn another language?
- Am I a good listener?
- Am I interested in helping people?
- Can I avoid feeling squeamish at the sight of blood or if someone's in pain?
- Can I make a commitment and follow it through?
- Am I willing to work hard?
- Can I work as part of a team?

To find out more about careers working with families contact:

American College of Nurse Midwives
1522 K Street, NW
Suite 1000
Washington, DC 20005

Association for the Care of Children's Health
7910 Woodmont Avenue
Suite 300
Bethesda, MD 20814

Association of Women's Health, Obstetric and Neonatal Nurses
409 12th Street, SW
Suite 300
Washington, DC 20024

The National Alliance of Nurse Practitioners
325 Pennsylvania Avenue, SE
Washington, DC 20003–1100

CAREERS

AS

COUNSELORS

Although you don't have to be an RN to find a
satisfying career in the mental health field, most
nurses feel they can better help people by taking
into account both physical and emotional factors.

As a counselor, you can choose a variety of settings in
which to work and a variety of people to see. You can
work in a hospital with psychiatric inpatients, for
example, or see clients in a clinic on an outpatient basis.
The work atmosphere and your duties will vary with the
setting.

The world of mental health counseling

In addition to RNs, a variety of other professionals work in the mental health field. Medical doctors can specialize in psychiatry, and then as psychiatrists, work full-time in a hospital or have a private practice with hospital privileges. This means that they are able to admit any of their patients who might need hospital care.

A psychologist does not attend medical school, but spends many years in college earning a PhD.

Psychotherapists, social workers, and family therapists usually have master's degrees and work in hospitals, private practice, or for government agencies.

Some settings—hospitals or government agencies, for example—also will employ mental health counselors with a bachelor's degree.

RNs and counseling

Registered nurses can work with emotionally disturbed patients or with patients who basically are well and just need support with normal problems. In order to make the right career choice, it is important to understand the type of work you would be doing. In a hospital setting you would deal with all types of patients. Many of them could be chronically ill without much hope for improvement. They could be severely depressed, suicidal, or violent and not be able to function in their normal lives.

Generally, in mental health clinics or health centers, patients will have less severe problems and the opportunities to help and see improvements are greater. You might work with clients going through a divorce, or grieving over the loss of a child or spouse.

Training for RN counselors

You need an RN as a minimum, and then your BSN. Some settings require further education and you could study for a master's degree in counseling, nursing, clinical psychology, or social work.

Counselors need to possess the following skills:

- Good people skills/the ability to interact well with people

- Good listening skills

- Tolerance toward people you don't understand

- Ability to be supportive and nurturing

- Flexibility
- Well-organized

Your work conditions

These vary depending upon the setting. RNs in a psychiatric hospital usually are paid on the same scale as floor nurses in other departments. Nurses working in health centers or clinics are generally paid more.

Hospital nurses often work more erratic hours—they can be scheduled for holidays, weekends, nights, evenings, and days. Nurses in a clinic have the benefit of more normal hours, Monday through Friday with only an occasional evening or weekend.

Hospital settings follow a "medical model," viewing the people they're helping as "patients" who are sick, relying on medication as a large segment of the therapy process.

Therapists in clinics view the people they are helping as basically well. Here they are called "clients." Therapy is more active, relying on talking, support, education, and working toward specific, achievable goals.

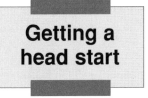

Getting a head start

You can start by getting involved in any peer counseling programs your school might offer. Later, you can volunteer and then find part-time work in a variety of mental health settings. During this process you will get a feel for what the work is like and you will be able to make an informed choice. You also will learn how to assess yourself and to see if you have what it takes.

Let's Meet...

Regina Renteria
Counselor, Educator, and Director of a Women's Health Center

Regina has been a nurse for 17 years and a counselor/ educator at a women's health center for 5 years. She loves being able to offer support and information to her clients.

Tell us about your clinic and the work you do there.

Our clinic is a department of a small community hospital. We're wellness-oriented, in that we deal mainly with a population of well women. We try to meet our client's health information needs and address their emotional well-being. We offer many different support groups. They're designed for women basically, because men often don't come to them. We have support groups for women who have had breast cancer. We have bereavement groups for widows, parents who have lost a child, or adults who have lost a parent. And we have a weekly domestic violence support and education group for women.

We help empower women by giving them support and information. Also, our clinic runs workshops on self-esteem, relationship skills, communication skills, assertiveness training, parenting, and adjustment to divorce. Our clients mostly are working and professional women, 35 to 55 years old.

Describe a typical day.

In the morning I might have a few one-on-one counseling sessions with clients, covering divorce or self-esteem issues. Then there's the administrative duties, the paperwork. I coordinate with other health care professionals and make referrals for my clients.

Also I give presentations in the community for a women's organization or a business. Right now, I'm working on a workshop for the postal service on managing anger. It's called "The Anger in You."

In the afternoon I attend a meeting or two then work on our newsletter, which we distribute to our clients. I have to read a lot, too. There's always new information coming into the clinic and I have to keep informed.

What do you like most, and least, about your job?

What I like most is getting to work with women who are well. In a hospital setting you can feel as if your efforts are not showing results, but in this kind of job you can feel you're making a difference. You can see your clients getting their needs met.

I like the idea of being independent. In my field you can collaborate with other professionals but you're not given a prescribed way of doing things. I can be very creative. I like everything about my job. I can't think of even one negative about it.

A Day with Christie Brinkley

Once a year at Regina Renteria's health center they invite famous speakers to talk to the community and to serve as role models. Among the celebrity guests they've hosted are Joan Rivers, Ivana Trump, Stephanie Powers, and Joan Lunden. But the person who impressed Regina the most was supermodel, Christie Brinkley.

Regina says Christie spoke about her life and her career. She's a vegetarian and an exercise fanatic, but she doesn't starve herself. Christie has a round, wholesome look to her, which was a new trend she set. She broke into modeling on the heels of the very skinny models.

She talked about what you see in the magazines. It's not real. There's a lot of touching up that goes on, but girls see these images and think that the models look like that all the time. It sets an impossible standard for them to follow.

Regina also got to know Christie more personally and discovered that she's very nice—down-to-earth, with a sensible outlook. She has a great sense of humor and can laugh at herself. She's interested in other people. Regina thinks she's an excellent role model.

Let's Meet...

Rob Verner
Psychiatric Nurse

Rob Verner has been a psychiatric nurse for more than 15 years. He works in an inpatient hospital setting and enjoys the one-on-one contact with his patients.

Tell us about where you work.

I work on three different units in my hospital. There's a psychiatric emergency room, where most of our patients are admitted, a short-term acute psychiatric unit for agitated patients, and a unit for adolescents age 10 to 18.

What kinds of problems do your patients have?

Some of them are depressed, even suicidal. Others suffer from schizophrenia, hear voices, or see things that aren't there. Some of the patients are violent. I can put on the nightly news before I come into work and hear about how the police apprehended a man waving a gun on the street. I know that when I get to work, he'll be there waiting for me.

The adolescents we get have severe problems at home, at school, or they're depressed or suicidal. Occasionally, we get an early schizophrenic who is starting to hear voices. That's very sad.

What made you decide to become a nurse?

When I was in college I had a work-study job at a state mental hospital. After I got out of college with my liberal arts degree, I wasn't sure what I wanted to do. I looked at all the jobs I'd had in my life and the one I liked the most was at the hospital. So I went and got another job similar to that one, but the pay was terrible. Someone suggested I become a nurse and I laughed. I had never considered it before. But then I thought about it some more and asked myself why not. So I did it.

I already had a bachelor's degree, in general studies, but there was a program at Case Western Reserve University for people just like me. I studied for 23 months straight and then earned my BSN.

Describe a typical day.

I read the report from the last shift. Then I greet all the patients I am assigned to. I discuss with them any special activities going on, with the recreational therapist or occupational therapist, for example. Later in the day I hand out medications, then talk with each patient about why they're in the hospital and how they're feeling.

I spend time setting limits and "redirecting" behavior. I find myself saying things like, "You can't go into that other patient's room, you need to stay in your own room or in the day room; you can't threaten to hit that person because you're angry with them; you have to put that chair down and not hit anybody with it." It's an acute unit and we have some violent patients.

A Memorable Patient

Rob Verner had a patient—a young, angry, high school student—who was having serious difficulties at home: an alcoholic father, brothers who were in trouble with the police, and one who had even ended up in prison.

This patient had broken into people's homes. One day he let himself into an apartment and sat down on the couch to wait for the residents to come home. He knew he needed help, but didn't know how to get it. He thought that by doing this, someone might help him.

The police came and took the young man to jail. He came to Rob's hospital to get treatment while they were waiting to decide what to do with him. He's the only kid Rob went to the courthouse for. He didn't belong in a detention home, he hadn't hurt anyone—he was looking for help.

The judge let him go and he stayed in the hospital for about two months. Rob spent a great deal of time working with him. They looked at the ineffective ways his brothers had dealt with their anger and how he needed to be smart and come up with a better plan—unless he wanted to go to prison, which was where he was heading.

Rob learned later that his patient finished high school, then went on to college and became a nurse.

Rob was happy he had done so well, and had turned his life around. Because he had chosen to become a nurse meant to Rob that perhaps he had helped him, and that he wanted to help other people in the same way.

Success Stories

Anna Freud

Anna Freud, born in 1895, was the daughter of Sigmund Freud, the "Father of Psychology." Anna Freud expanded upon her father's work and became a pioneer in the field of child psychoanalysis. She devoted much effort to the welfare of children. After leaving Vienna to work in London, she founded the Hampstead War Nurseries and the Hampstead Child Therapy Course and Clinic. Anna Freud died in 1982.

Jean Piaget

Jean Piaget was one of the most influential experimenters in the study of human intelligence. His main area of interest was how children learn, perhaps because he was a genius himself and had an unusual childhood.

Piaget published his first scientific paper at the age of 10, on observations of an albino sparrow he had discovered near his home. He had an after-school job working at a local natural history museum in his native Switzerland. This job led him to write a series of articles on mollusks. The articles led to a sight-unseen invitation to become a curator at a museum in Geneva. Piaget turned down the job offer so he could finish high school.

Find Out More

You and counseling

Test Your Self-Esteem

A good level of self-esteem is
important to the health of your
clients—and to your own emotional well-being.

How high is your self-esteem?
Answer the questions TRUE or
FALSE, then turn the page to find
your rating.

	TRUE	FALSE
1. I feel warm and happy toward myself.		
2. I speak up for my own opinions.		
3. I do my own thinking and make my own decisions.		
4. I take responsibility for the consequences of my actions.		
5. I feel free to express love, anger, joy, resentment, and all my other emotions.		
6. I rarely experience jealousy, envy, or suspicion.		
7. I don't feel put down or rejected if someone disagrees with me.		
8. I admit my mistakes, shortcomings, and defeats.		
9. I can make and keep friends without exerting myself.		
10. Everything doesn't always have to be perfect.		
11. I accept compliments and gifts without embarrassment.		
12. I am friendly, considerate, and generous with others.		

Your self-esteem rating

The more questions you were able to answer with TRUE, the better your self-esteem is. Count up your TRUE answers, then find your score below.

0 to 4   You need to work on your self-esteem. Talk to an adult you trust about the things that concern you.

5 to 8   Your self-esteem is not too bad, but there are still areas you could work on. Again, discuss your concerns with a parent, a counselor, or a teacher at school.

9 to 12   Congratulations. Your self-esteem is excellent. You are confident, mature, and you can take care of yourself!

To learn more about counseling contact:

Advocates for Child Psychiatric Nursing
437 Twin Bay Drive
Pensacola, FL 32534

Society for Education and Research in Psychiatric-Mental Health Nursing
437 Twin Bay Drive
Pensacola, FL 32534

CAREERS

IN

EDUCATION

S ome people consider a career in nursing education to be the most important path a nurse could
follow. If no one was interested in teaching future
nurses, eventually there would be no more nurses.

But nursing education encompasses even more than
training RNs or BSNs. To some extent, every nurse is
involved with education. Nurses educate and learn from
each other and pass vital information on to their
patients and their communities.

With enough education, many diseases could be cured
or, even more important, prevented. A properly trained

nurse will provide better care for his or her patients. A properly educated patient will reduce the risks of getting sick again in the future. Education improves the overall quality of life for everyone.

Where nurse educators find work

Nurses who become teachers can find work in a variety of settings. They can teach future nurses in hospital training programs, in two-year community colleges, in four-year colleges and universities, and in master's and doctorate programs. They also can work in technical schools in programs that prepare licensed practical nurses (LPNs) or in a large hospital, welcoming newly em-ployed nurses with orientation and training to hospital procedures.

In addition to training nurses, nurse educators work with patients, providing information and instruction on a variety of subjects. They might work in a patient's home, in a private doctor's office, a clinic or women's health care center, in a hospital outpatient department, on an isolated Indian reservation, or in a rural farming community. These educators help patients with preventative health care, family planning, or the proper management of certain illnesses. For example, a nurse educator could help people with diabetes understand their disease and train them how to self-administer their medication.

The training you'll need

The qualifications you'll need depends upon where and at what level you'll be teaching. To teach future nurses in a university setting you will need your BSN to start with, but you must go on to earn your master's degree and then a PhD in nursing. A doctorate program can take from three to five years after your four-year BSN program. In addition to earning your degrees, you will need to have some practical experience as a "hands-on" nurse.

Most other settings where you will be working as an educator don't require the doctorate degree. A BSN and a master's degree in nursing or social work will be sufficient to provide orientation and training to nurses just starting a new job or to provide information and health education to patients in a women's health clinic. In any case, before you can teach others, you must be experienced.

The rewards, the pay, and the perks

Traditionally, educators have been the lowest paid professionals. First-year nurses graduating with a BSN will earn more than their professors do. A nurse can make more money outside an educational setting. Those who decide to follow a career in nursing education obviously are not doing it for the money. Salaries are more generous in hospitals for nurse educators providing orientation and training to newly employed nurses.

Although the pay might be low, the hours are a plus for most educators. They might work a 40-hour week, but those hours are not all spent in the classroom and there is a satisfying amount of variety to their duties.

The pleasures and pressures of the job

For many nursing educators, the main pleasure of the profession is seeing someone come in not knowing anything about the field, molding them, and then years later learning through a visit, a call, or a letter the difference they made in their lives. The reward comes from being a mentor.

The main pressure for nursing educators is that they have to keep on their toes at all times. They have to stay informed about all the new nursing procedures, new equipment, new policies, and regulations. It's up to them to pass on current information to their students—things are changing constantly.

They also have the pressure of attending to the various needs of all their students or patients. The demands can be physically and emotionally draining, but the pleasures and rewards more than make up for it.

The job outlook

In the past, most nurses earned their RN through a three-year hospital-based training program. These programs are being phased out slowly and more nurses go directly into a four-year university to earn their BSN. This means that there will be more openings at the university level for nurse educators. Universities already are having difficulty recruiting enough teachers because of the low pay received by nursing educators. If you decide you would like to teach, and you've completed your higher degrees and have practiced in the field for several years, chances are you'll be able to find a job at the institution of your choice.

Let's Meet...

Betty Clay
Nurse Educator

Betty has been a nurse for over 30 years and a nurse educator for 8 years. She has an RN and a bachelor's degree in health services.

Tell us about your job.

I go over all the paperwork with the new nurses. I explain our forms and our method of charting, because that does vary from hospital to hospital. We cover pre- and post-operative procedures, so nurses know how to assess patients when they come from surgery. In addition, we have a floor for terminal patients and cancer patients and we train new nurses on the special precautions there.

Because I have nurses coming on board with a variety of backgrounds—critical care, obstetrics, some brand new nurses—I gear the orientation to the basics, so when they appear on the floor in their uniform ready to work they understand how to chart, how to dispense medications, how to collect specimens, and how to start IVs, among other things.

I go over procedures and equipment for an emergency situation. I bring the crash cart in—it looks like a tool box—and

point out all the items in every drawer. They
need to know about the protocols for calling
an emergency—what we call a "Code One"
here.

Also I teach classes in CPR for nurses,
nursing assistants, and for unit secretaries.

What do you like most about your job?

What I like most is meeting new personnel
because they're eager and enthusiastic. For
many people it's their first job, sometimes
even a whole new career, and I enjoy working with them. They're so excited, wanting
to get started and learn as much as they can.

I like that I get to know all the areas of
the hospital. As a bedside nurse you know
only the floor you're working on. But I get to
become familiar with all the different
departments. I've met a lot of interesting
people and it's broadened my knowledge.

My hours are a lot better than when I was
a floor nurse, too. It's a day shift job, no
nights. I work Monday through Friday 8 to
4:30, weekends off, holidays off, which you
don't see when you work on the floor. And I
don't have to wear a uniform.

What do you like least?

That's easy. I miss working with the
patients. I think any nurse would. That's
why you go into nursing, to have the hands-
on contact.

There's also the deadlines. I have many
deadlines for providing orientations on a
schedule and for getting all the paperwork
in on time for new hirees.

A Surprise Meeting for Betty

When Betty Clay first began her career in nursing she worked on a medical-surgical floor. She tells us here about a special patient and the surprise he gave her. Betty worked with patients who had just come back from surgery. During those first hours they're very dependent on a nurse; they're sleeping a lot and may be frightened or disoriented. And usually, they're appreciative of the care given them. Having an operation can be a real ordeal. But it's rare for a nurse to ever see them again.

Years later, Betty was having a garage sale and a man stopped by. He saw her and her children, and before she realized who he was, he started telling them how wonderful she had been to him, what a wonderful person she was. Betty never had anybody come back later on and say "thank you very much, you did a lot for me, I couldn't have got through it without you." Her children looked at her with new eyes. They knew Betty was a nurse, but they hadn't thought about what she did, how she helped people. The experience was overwhelming; Betty wasn't prepared for it, hadn't expected it, but it felt great.

Let's Meet...

Jill Winland-Brown
Associate Professor of Nursing

Jill is a nurse and a doctor— a doctor of education! She teaches future nurses at Florida Atlantic University. She has been an RN for 25 years and a university teacher for 13 years.

What's your job like?

There are three components to my work: teaching, service, and research.

I teach clinical and theory courses such as nursing ethics, leadership management, and technological skills (giving medications, starting IVs, etc.) 12 hours a week. In addition, there's preparing lessons and grading papers.

The service part of my job means giving something back to the community and to the university. I serve on many boards and committees. I advise undergraduate and graduate students and help them with their independent studies, theses, or dissertations.

When you're a professor you're expected to do research, to further your own knowledge and that of others in important areas. Some of my research topics have been problems for disabled nurses and summer camp nursing. You write papers to report what you've learned and you submit these papers to professional journals for publication.

How did you get started—and how can others?

I started in a three-year diploma program and got my RN. I worked for seven years and then went back to earn my bachelor's, my master's, and then my doctorate. I worked as a nurse throughout my studies.

These days it's much better to start out directly in a bachelor's program; it will take you less time. And though right now nurses all take the same licensing exam, in a few years that will change. There will be a technical level and a professional level exam; only the BSN graduate will be at the professional level. If you want to teach, or even if you don't and you want to practice any other area of nursing, you should study for your bachelor's degree. It will be the entry into professional practice and will open many more doors for you.

What do you like most about your job?

I like working with a wide range of students—whether they're freshmen, seniors, or master's level students or RNs coming back to earn their bachelor's degree. I'm an advisor to many students, too. They're assigned to me when they first begin and they stay with me all the way through their program. I like being able to follow them through their education and to get to know them well.

I also enjoy being near people who are working in a variety of disciplines. Most hospital nurses work only with other health care professionals. In a university setting you come in contact with all different kinds of people.

Because I Care...

This poem was written by one of Jill Winland-Brown's students to share his feelings about nursing with others. It first appeared in *Nightingale Songs,* a publication edited by a Florida Atlantic University College of Nursing faculty member.

Because I care, I bring
    hope to your hopelessness,
Because I care, I see you
    as loving woman and mother.

Because I care, I enter
    your world with humility and respect
I honor your belief that
    somehow I can help.
I live your caring with you,
    to cry when sad
    to howl with delight.

Because I care, I want to
    be there with you and for you
    in sharing your pain and joy.

Because you care, I can
    care with you
Caring creates meaning for you and I.

        by Daniel L. Little

Success Stories

Many of you have read about Helen Keller or seen *The Miracle Worker,* the inspiring movie of her life. She was born in 1880 and at the age of 19 months, because of a brain fever, became blind and deaf. She could communicate only through hysterical laughter or violent tantrums. Her family hired a teacher for her, Anne Sullivan, who led Helen out of darkness into a fulfilling life.

Anne Sullivan taught Helen how to read braille and to write by using a special typewriter. Later, Helen attended Radcliffe College, Harvard University's sister school, and graduated with honors. Her unusual life and dedicated work had an international influence on the lives of the handicapped. She wrote books, lectured, and raised money to help those in need. Helen Keller died in 1968.

Find Out More

You and nursing education

Do you have what it takes to be a nursing educator? Ask yourself the following questions to find out:

- Will I be willing to spend up to eight or nine years studying to achieve my goal?
- Will I be willing to work as a floor nurse or in any other nursing area to gain experience before I go on to teach?
- Will I be content with a salary lower than the nurses I am training?

If you answered "yes" to all three questions, this might be the career for you. But to know for sure, you will have to spend time exploring all the different nursing options. Time and experience will lead you in the right direction.

Find out more about nurse educators

Association of Community Health
  Nursing Educators
c/o 64 Neron Place
New Orleans, LA 70118

National Nursing Staff
  Development Organization
  (NNSD)
437 Twin Bay Drive
Pensacola, FL 32534

The NNSD is open to nurses engaged in any aspect of nursing staff education.

CAREERS
IN
ADMINISTRATION

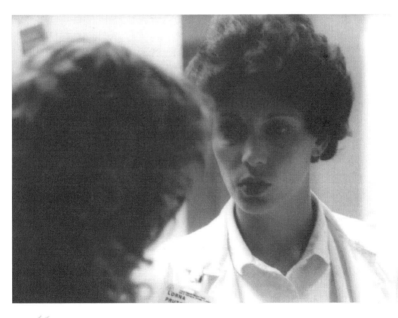

B ecause of health reform, health administration is widening up for nurses beyond the acute-care hospital. There will be many different facilities—a variety of clinics, hospices, family planning centers, and HMOs—where nursing administrators will find satisfying employment. If you have any of the qualities of a leader or manager, then a job in administration could be for you.

What it's like being a nursing administrator

There are nursing administrative positions at a variety of levels—from charge nurse to the top executive spot in a hospital or clinic. Depending upon which rung you find yourself on the ladder, your duties could involve little or no direct patient care. Most nursing administrators supervise the work of other nurses and hospital staff, such as unit secretaries, nursing assistants, and aids. Some administrators provide training to new nurses or advise student nurses.

Other duties include managing budgets, hiring and firing staff, scheduling shifts, and working out any problems that may arise. Also, administrators spend much of their time attending meetings and sitting on committees.

The rewards, the pay, and the perks

In addition to a high degree of job satisfaction, most administrators find the financial compensation to be more than fair. Depending upon the setting and your rank, your salary could range from $30,000 to $125,000 a year.

Some hospitals have profit-sharing or offer their employees annual bonuses. Most are unable to afford this and nursing administrators receive their salaries and a package of benefits that includes health and dental insurance, vacation days, holidays, and sick leave. Many have a budget for continuing education and you could be financed to attend conferences and seminars or to take more college courses.

Pleasures and pressures of the job

A job in health administration can be satisfying. It's motivating if you feel that you can accomplish something, especially if you have a supportive administrator at the top. You can carry on things within your own department the way you want to.

There's a tremendous amount of work that goes along with that, but good administrators are prepared to handle the pressure; most even thrive on it. But there are some pressures administrators could do without. One of them is the cost of health care. It's never pleasant to have to reduce staff or eliminate a department to keep costs down, for example. At the same time, you want to continue to give quality care to patients, and you have to fight for the money to do it sometimes, and validate your needs to the administrators above you.

The training you'll need

These days, most new nurse administrators must have a master's degree in addition to the BSN. The master's could be in nursing, business administration, health management, or any related field. This course of study could take from one to two years above the BSN.

In addition, a nurse administrator, in order to be effective, must have a good deal of practical experience working as a nurse. It would be difficult, if not impossible, to manage a clinic, or a floor, department, or hospital without first having experienced its day-to-day workings.

Getting ahead

Once you've had your hands-on practical training, and have finished your master's degree, you might not automatically be promoted from a clinical position to an administrative one. Opportunities in your work setting could be limited, with no openings for nurse manager, or higher, available. When that happens, a nurse who wants to move ahead would have to move on. That could be as easy as moving to another clinic or hospital in your city, or as difficult as relocating to another state. There are more staff and floor nurse positions than there are spots for the nurses who supervise them.

Is administration right for you?

Most people choose nursing as a career because they want to help other people. Some prefer working with critically ill patients, others prefer helping a healthy population. But most nursing administrators find that the higher up the ladder they go, the less time they have to spend with patients.

Administrators still deal with people; they spend a lot of their time communicating with other staff members or colleagues. Sometimes they interact with the patients' families. Some might even go into the community and work with other professionals in related organizations, such as a community health care board or neighborhood health center.

Administrators must be good leaders. They have to be fair and show good judgment. Also they have to be sensitive to the needs of their staff. Administrators carry a lot of responsibility and they can't be afraid to make important decisions.

And don't forget the paperwork, meetings, and phone calls. Administrators have to be good jugglers, trying to meet all the demands on their time.

Let's Meet...

Edie Quinn
Nurse Manager

Edie Quinn has been the nurse manager in a hospital intensive care unit for more than 20 years. She feels that being a nurse manager offers a constant challenge.

What drew you to nursing?

I started working as a nurse's assistant and I received much satisfaction as the patients' illnesses improved. So I investigated nursing as a career and discovered a profession with a good job outlook, good salaries, and the opportunity to combine several different skills. I could be a nurse, a teacher, and a manager. Plus, there was the opportunity to express to other people that no matter what their problems were, there was someone there who wanted to help.

What made you decide to go into nurse management?

Actually, a physician encouraged me. He thought I was capable and that I could handle it. I wavered for about six months, then I decided to give it a whirl and accept the promotion. And, I went on to study for a degree in professional management while I continued to work full-time.

What does a nurse manager do?

I organize, plan, and evaluate care that is given to patients, and I manage the entire 16-bed unit. Also, I supervise 52 nurses, tracking their performance, their time and attendance and whether they're tardy, and their documentation, to be sure they write everything they do in the patients' chart.

The biggest part is the scheduling. I have to make sure the shifts are covered and that all 52 nurses work the number of days they're supposed to and get the number of holidays and vacation days they're entitled to. I hire and fire nurses, handle the budget, and make sure the physicians have everything they need to work with.

Although I do make patient rounds everyday and interact with their families, there's very little hands-on patient contact; basically, my job is management.

What do you like most/least about your job?

I like the interaction with my staff and people in other departments. Also I like to encourage my staff with their careers, to help them grow and advance.

There aren't too many downsides because I enjoy what I do. The only thing would be personalities and having to deal with all the different types. Also, trying to satisfy all the physicians with their little quirks. You have to be tolerant.

Edie's First Day on the Job

The entire staff knew she was going to be coming to the unit the next day as the head nurse, which is what nurse managers were called then. Because she's Black they had some questions or concerns. Edie didn't really know what they were, but she found out in an unusual way.

That first morning as she was making rounds with one of the physicians, a patient said to her, "Even though I've never met you, I know you, because I heard all about you last night." He then went on to relate all the gossip to the doctor, as if she weren't standing there. The doctor was concerned that she would feel discouraged, but she didn't. Edie understood that it's normal to worry about a new manager coming onboard—it's the fear of the unknown and she was prepared for it.

Later that day, when Edie met with the staff, she told them that she was available to them and if they had any problems they could come talk to her about them. It eased the tension and the rest of the day went well.

Head Nurse

Let's Meet...

Julie Benthal
Vice President of Nursing

Julie has been a nurse for close to 45 years. For the last few years she has been the top nursing administrator at a community hospital.

What made you decide to become a nurse?

I just wanted to care for patients. If I had been born a little later I would have gone to medical school, but back then becoming a doctor was not an easy route for women to take. Before becoming the Vice President of Nursing, I worked in critical care for years taking care of very ill patients. I loved it.

How did you get started with nursing administration?

I started accumulating administrative experience when I was a student nurse. I worked as a charge nurse then, and over the years I moved up through the ranks, from nurse manager to where I am now.

What are your duties as Vice President of Nursing?

I'm responsible for nursing throughout the hospital. I attend all sorts of meetings and I'm on long-range planning and budget

committees. It's a way of communicating and knowing what's going on in the hospital. For example, I meet with all the nurse managers once a month. We look at how we can ensure the best possible patient care and try to resolve any ongoing concerns.

In addition to overseeing staffing and schedules, I'm responsible for a hefty $20 million budget for the division of nursing. Also I'm on the advisory board for student nurses. It's busy, but I enjoy it.

What do you find most satisfying about your work?

You can work with the nursing profession and see it grow and develop. With health reform a lot of creative innovation is going on right now. Hospitals and staffing are being re-organized to better meet the needs of the patients. It's called patient-centered care.

People are rethinking the way they work—not just nursing, but all the depart-ments. It's a much more collaborative team effort. The idea of health reform is to give better care that is less costly.

I find it rewarding that I get a chance to network, sharing ideas and information. There's a lot of flexibility and a lot of chal-lenge. It's never boring.

What's the most difficult aspect of your job?

What I don't like is fighting for more staff. That's a problem that comes up once a year when we're dealing with budgets.

A Pyramid of Nurses

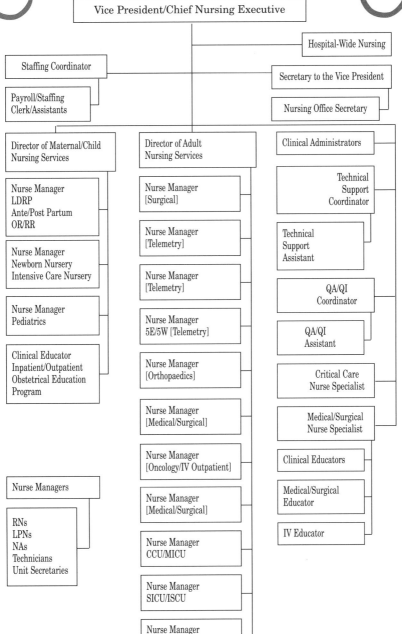

Vice President/Chief Nursing Executive

Hospital-Wide Nursing

Staffing Coordinator

Secretary to the Vice President

Payroll/Staffing Clerk/Assistants

Nursing Office Secretary

Director of Maternal/Child Nursing Services

Director of Adult Nursing Services

Clinical Administrators

Nurse Manager LDRP Ante/Post Partum OR/RR

Nurse Manager [Surgical]

Technical Support Coordinator

Nurse Manager [Telemetry]

Technical Support Assistant

Nurse Manager Newborn Nursery Intensive Care Nursery

Nurse Manager [Telemetry]

Nurse Manager Pediatrics

Nurse Manager 5E/5W [Telemetry]

QA/QI Coordinator

QA/QI Assistant

Clinical Educator Inpatient/Outpatient Obstetrical Education Program

Nurse Manager [Orthopaedics]

Critical Care Nurse Specialist

Nurse Manager [Medical/Surgical]

Medical/Surgical Nurse Specialist

Nurse Manager [Oncology/IV Outpatient]

Clinical Educators

Nurse Managers

Nurse Manager [Medical/Surgical]

Medical/Surgical Educator

RNs LPNs NAs Technicians Unit Secretaries

Nurse Manager CCU/MICU

IV Educator

Nurse Manager SICU/ISCU

Nurse Manager Dialysis

Success Stories

The Mayo Clinic

Dr. William Worrall Mayo came to Rochester, Minnesota, from England and settled there as a country doctor, later to become the head of St. Mary's Hospital. His two sons grew up to become distinguished surgeons who formed the Mayo Clinic as part of St. Mary's in the early 1900s.

At first it was only a small surgical clinic, but the two brothers quickly expanded it and brought in famous physicians from around the world. Dr. William Mayo's grandson also became a skilled surgeon and served on the governing board of the clinic.

Now the Mayo Clinic has a worldwide reputation and has over 900 physicians and surgeons on staff.

The Nobel Prize

When Alfred Nobel died, he left most of his large fortune in a trust fund from which annual prizes could be awarded. He wanted the prizes to be given to "those who conferred the greatest benefit on mankind."

The prizes designated in Nobel's will were for physics, chemistry, literature, peace, and medicine. Later, economics was added.

The average value of each prize has grown from $90,000 in 1901 to about $1.2 million in 1992. Up to three people can share the prize, and several people, including Marie Curie, have won the prize twice.

Find Out More

You and nursing adminis- tration

Many nursing specialties require that you earn a master's degree after your BSN. College students, both undergraduate (studying for a bachelor's degree) and graduate (studying for a master's or doctoral degree) take between 12 and 20 classroom hours each week, depending on their program. In class they listen to the instructor and take notes. At home, they study textbooks, write research papers, and prepare for tests.

Graduate students also have to write a long research paper called a thesis or dissertation. Their instructors advise them through the many steps.

Most programs will also have some sort of clinical component. This means you will get hands-on training in a hospital or other clinical setting.

These are some of the subjects you would study in a master's degree program leading to a career in nursing administration.

- Budgeting
- Clinical management
- Economics
- Finance
- Health law

- Personnel management/Human resources
- Psychology
- Quality assurance
- Strategic planning

To find out more about nursing administration contact:

The American Organization of Nurse Executives
840 North Lake Shore Drive
Chicago, IL 60611

Council on Graduate Education
for Administration in Nursing
Duquesne University
630 College Hall
Pittsburgh, PA 15282

NURSES

ON THE GO

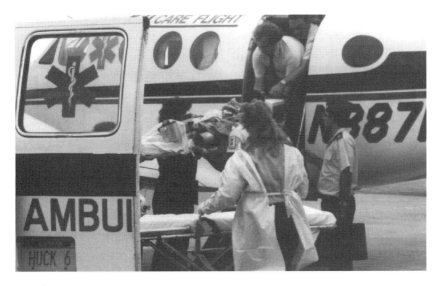

N ot all nurses work in hospitals or wear the traditional white uniform—approximately 32 percent of all nurses work in a setting other than a
hospital. Some find employment in unusual places—
lakeside at a summer camp, on an Indian reservation, or
aboard a cruise ship. And some nurses find interesting
and unusual patients to work with: military personnel,
world class marathon runners, ice skaters, or professional football players, to name just a few.

In this chapter we will meet two nurses who have
chosen uncommon work settings that keep them on the

go. One works in a sports medicine clinic treating professional ballet dancers and athletes; the other travels
the world to exotic places, working for the United States
government with the Foreign Service.

If being tied to a hospital routine doesn't appeal to
you, but the chance to meet interesting people and
travel to tempting destinations does, then consider some
of the following possibilities.

Job settings for nurses on the go

The Armed Forces: Nurses find
work in the army, navy, marines,
air force, and coast guard. They
enter with an officer's ranking
and receive all the privileges of
that rank. They could be posted
at bases and hospitals within the
United States, aboard ship, or at
U.S. bases overseas.

Cruise Ships: Everyone, at one
time or another, has seen reruns
of "The Love boat" on television
and watched Doc, Julie, Issac,
Gopher, and Captain Steubing
interact with passengers, having
fun while ensuring that everyone
has the best vacation possible.

Although the reality might not
mirror life on the popular series,
being part of a cruise ship staff
can be fun and exciting, with the
opportunity to travel to exotic
ports, meet all different kinds of
people, make new friends, and
lead a carefree lifestyle. The
downside is that shipboard nurses
can work long hours and be away
from home for weeks at a time.

The Foreign Service: A career
serving your country overseas can
offer excitement, challenge, and
even glamour. As a member of the
Foreign Service, which is under
the jurisdiction of the United
States Department of State, you
can travel the world, and, at the
same time, gain the satisfaction of
helping other people and repre-
senting the interests of your
country.

Being a part of the Foreign
Service is more than just a job. It
is a complete way of life that
requires dedication and commitment. If you're smart enough to
get the job done, the Foreign
Service might just be the right
place for you.

Foreign Service Officers can be
based in Washington, DC, or can
be sent anywhere in the world.
They work at embassies, consu-
lates, and other diplomatic mis-
sions in major cities or small towns.
Nurses with the Foreign Service
usually are appointed to an
American embassy and attend to
U.S. diplomats and their families.

The Peace Corps: The Peace
Corps offers interesting opportunities for adults of all ages,
though most new recruits are
recent college graduates. Place-
ments are for a two-year period.
Payment covers training, medical
expenses, and transportation.

There is no salary as such, but monthly allowances pay for food, lodging, and incidentals.

Peace Corps nurses are expected to be qualified in their field. They work in a variety of settings, from rural or traveling clinics, to city hospitals. The training and experience received while in the Peace Corps look impressive on any nurse's resume.

The Red Cross: Nurses in the Red Cross can work at home, in neighborhood clinics, teaching first aid and CPR, or be on the front line helping casualties in a war zone or in the aftermath of a hurricane or earthquake.

Sports Medicine: Sports medicine nurses work in clinics, some hospitals, training rooms, rehabilitation centers, outpatient centers, and school infirmaries. Some nurses work at first aid stations at the various sporting events. Often they work as part of a team—with physicians, surgeons, and physical therapists.

Sports medicine nurses attend to both professional and amateur athletes, from Olympic ice skaters and professional ballet dancers, to the neighborhood soccer or Little League team.

Summer Camps: RNs can enjoy their summer and earn money too, working with children in a healthy outdoor setting at overnight or day camps. Their duties could range from simple first-aid or treating insect bites, to setting broken bones or teaching water safety.

The perks at a summer camp are all those the campers enjoy: fresh air, clean lakes to swim and boat in, tennis, horseback riding, and other fun activities.

What it's like on the go

On-the-go nurses, especially those who travel overseas, need to be flexible and willing to adapt to a new environment. Life in a foreign country might not be similar to anything you are used to at home in the U.S. People react differently, rules and laws are different, the sights and sounds and even the smells are different. And most difficult for some nurses to become adjusted to is that medical facilities and medical practices might not meet American standards. Your hospital in a rural village in West Africa could be a tin-roofed hut with no electricity or running water. Medication could be scarce, as well as food and other important supplies. And there's always the danger of political unrest or war.

On the lighter side, on-the-go nurses usually benefit from all their experiences and the people they meet. For them, the true rewards are all the different challenges they face and overcome every day.

Let's Meet...

Bobbie Campbell
Sports Medicine Nurse

Bobbie works in a private sports medicine clinic that is owned by a physician and a physical therapist. She has been a sports nurse for nearly 25 years.

Can you give us a definition of sports medicine?

Sports medicine is a subspecialty of orthopedic medicine and deals primarily with injuries received during athletic activities. Sports medicine nurses care for patients suffering from strains, sprains, torn ligaments and muscles, fractures, and dislocations. Patients could be Little League shortstops, professional ballet dancers, ice skaters, aerobics exercisers, or marathon runners. Anyone with an active lifestyle can suffer a sports-related injury. It's the job of the sports medicine nurse to take a patient's history, assist the doctor with his or her treatment plan, and to educate the patient so future injuries can be avoided.

Tell us about a typical day.

I work about 36 hours a week. My hours can vary but they're usually Monday through Friday. I can arrive at 7 A.M. to a full schedule of patients. I'll escort them to the exam room, take a history and do

a brief screening. If necessary, I'll take their blood pressure and interview them about how they got their injury. I work with the doctor and when he goes to examine a patient I go with him. I write down every-thing he says and take notes for the patient. After the doctor leaves the room, I go over everything the doctor told the patient—the diagnosis, the plan for treatment, and what they're supposed to do at home. I might give him samples of medication and explain the side effects—there's a great deal of explana-tion to the patient. Also, if needed, I might give an injection or take an x-ray.

What are some of the pleasures—and the pressures—of your job?

The pleasures are numerous. You have patient contact and deal with a healthy and well-motivated population. I like being able to share knowledge and educate people to prevent injuries.

The hours are pleasurable—much better than hospital work. The job is varied, there are many different aspects to it. I work with different age groups and get to incorporate the general knowledge I learned in my nursing program. You can take your educa-tion and skills and use them often. And you get to go to the ballet and sporting events.

The only pressure I can think of is that most of the patients are in a hurry to get well. They're anxious to get back to their sport, and they want to get back *now!* That can be a great incentive, but it also can be a pressure. Bodies can heal only so quickly.

A Day at the Races

The Goodwill Games came to Bobbie's hometown of Seattle, Washington, a couple of years ago and her clinic and other health professionals in the community were invited to participate.

Like the Olympics, the Goodwill Games is an international competition held in various sites around the world, and they attract an elite level of athlete. Bobbie was asked to work with the marathon runners.

When the winners crossed the finish line, they needed emergency medical assistance—it was a hot day. Bobbie and the other health care professionals treated the runners for heat exhaustion, ankle strains, and blisters. There were a lot of blisters.

Bobbie noted that one of the women top finishers was from Russia and couldn't speak English. She wanted some kind of medication and it took a while to figure out she just needed an aspirin.

The woman came back later on after the award ceremony just to say thank you. That's what made it so rewarding. Here they were, elite athletes competing in this important event, fulfilling a lifelong dream of theirs, yet they still thought to come back and thank the volunteers.

Bobbie said that it was nice to be appreciated and realized that we are all people, no matter what country we're from. Providing care is universal.

Let's Meet...

Shirley Panasuk
Foreign Service Nurse

Shirley has worked as a nurse in U.S. embassies in a variety of exotic places, including Moscow and Baghdad. Currently, she is posted in Ankara, Turkey.

What is it like working for the Foreign Service?

There are two types of nurses who work in the Foreign Service: nurse practitioners and contract nurses. I am a contract nurse for the Department of State in a position they call "PIT." That stands for Part-time, Intermittent, Temporary. My patients are the diplomats working in the U.S. embassy and their dependents.

The job is challenging and always different, depending on which country you're posted in. I worked as a nurse in the embassy in Baghdad during the Iran-Iraq war, and for the first couple of years we didn't have a hospital for our patients. The people really depended on me there.

Now I work in Ankara part-time sharing a job with another nurse so we can keep up our skills. In addition, I volunteer at a clinic in a village outside Ankara and serve on the Ankara International Charities Committee. Each year we have four events to raise money to buy equipment for schools, hospitals,

and clinics in Turkey, and clothing for Turkish children.

I take care of all sorts of problems—flu, sore throats, and injuries—but I don't do any diagnosing. We have a regional doctor based in Athens. Regional doctors can cover more than nine or ten countries. He has to give us permission for many different things but he does rely on my judgment. I can call him up and tell him I think someone needs to be medically evacuated (flown out of the country to a U.S. hospital) and he gives his approval based on what I tell him. And if one of our patients has to be admitted to a local hospital, I'm in touch with him by cable, fax, or phone.

What are your duties?

My day usually starts out with the phone ringing, with someone who has had some problem during the night. The nurse I work with and I do a lot of encouraging and listening. People will come to us with a sore throat, for example, and we'll take a culture and send it to the lab. If it comes back negative, then I assume it's viral and they'll get over it. I instruct them to gargle and drink lots of liquids. However, if a person needs to be on antibiotics, we have a local doctor who can prescribe the medication.

If someone has to go to the local hospital, I escort them there and stay with them throughout all the tests to reassure them. It can be very frightening to be alone in a hospital, in a foreign country when you don't speak the language.

A Simple Act of Kindness

While volunteering at a village clinic near Ankara, Turkey, Shirley saw many nursing practices that disturbed her. She felt that the nurses in Turkey did not receive as much training as they should have.

Every day there would be many patients in the waiting room, all bundled up in layers of clothing because it was cold outside and few homes had heat. The Turkish nurses, when they had to take a blood pressure, placed the cuff over all the layers. They didn't talk to their patients, reassure them, or try to make them comfortable.

There was one patient Shirley remembers particularly. Shirley helped her to undress so she could take her blood pressure on her bare arm and then asked her about her health.

When Shirley escorted her to the doctor's office, the woman was amazed to find a doctor there. She had thought that Shirley was the doctor. When she learned that Shirley was an American nurse volunteering at the clinic, the woman beamed. She thanked Shirley over and over for her kindness.

Shirley felt touched that such a simple act would be so appreciated.

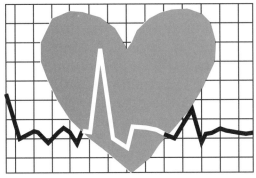

Success Stories

The Red Cross   Whenever there's a natural disaster—earthquakes, floods, hurricanes, etc.—at home, or in some far away country, the Red Cross seems to be the first relief organization on the scene. And in countries torn by war, the Red Cross is there to help all the victims.

The men and women who work for the Red Cross are brave and dedicated health professionals. By maintaining a political neutrality, they are able to enter countries in conflict. But even though the red cross painted on rooftops and flown on flags is supposed to warn away any hostile armies, they are still targets.

Jean Henri Dunant, from Switzerland, founded the International Red Cross in 1881.

In addition to natural disasters and war relief, the Red Cross also teaches courses in first aid and water safety, helps refugees, and maintains blood banks.

Blood Banks   Blood banks are facilities where blood is collected, stored, and processed for later use during operations and whenever a blood transfusion is required. The first blood bank was formed in 1937 at Cook County Hospital in Chicago. Today, most blood is collected at regional and community centers that then provide it to regional hospitals, although some large hospitals collect their own blood. The Red Cross runs most of these regional blood banks.

Find Out More

Caps and Pins: The Symbols of Nursing

The cap and pin have long been symbols of the profession of nursing. Every nursing school has its own design, and student nurses look forward to the day they graduate and are given the privilege of wearing both.

Caps were used initially to cover the hair for sanitary purposes when working with seriously ill patients; the black band around some caps was used to distinguish graduates from students and supervisors from staff. These days, the black band has lost its significance and many nurses, especially those working outside a hospital setting, have discarded the custom of wearing the cap altogether.

But the school pin nurses are given upon graduation still remains as an identifying badge worn with pride. Many pins incorporate the symbol of different crosses. The Red Cross uses St. George's Cross—blood red on a field of white. That cross has stood for unselfish service for centuries. It was chosen with the politically neutral country, Switzerland, in mind. The Red Cross flag bears the colors of Switzerland in reverse.

Other nursing pin crosses
symbolize relief (Lorraine cross),
purity (Maltese cross), protection
of the weak (Pattee cross),
support (Latin cross), humility
(St. Andrew's cross), and mercy
and life (Tau cross).

**To find out
more about
on-the-go
nursing
careers
contact:**

American College of Sports
  Medicine (ACSM)
Member and Chapter Services
  Department
P.O. Box 1440
Indianapolis, IN 46206

American Red Cross
National Headquarters
17th & D Streets, NW
Washington, DC 20006

Foreign Service
Department of State
Recruitment Division
P.O. Box 9317
Rosslyn Station
Arlington, VA 22209

Peace Corps
Box 941
Washington, DC 20526

INDEX